# One Little, Two Little, Three Little Apples

To Nat & Annette and Tony & Bobby — for all the great autumn memories
— M.R.

For Robin and Connie, my apple-picking pals

— A.K.

ISBN 0-439-77500-0

Text copyright © 2005 by Matt Ringler
Illustrations copyright © 2005 by Anne Kennedy

12 11 10 9 8 7 6 5 4 3 2          5 6 7 8 9 10/0

Printed in the U.S.A.
First printing, October 2005

# One Little, Two Little, Three Little Apples

by Matt Ringler

Illustrations by Anne Kennedy

SCHOLASTIC INC.

New York  Toronto  London  Auckland  Sydney
Mexico City  New Delhi  Hong Kong  Buenos Aires

1 little, 2 little, 3 little apples,

4 little, 5 little, 6 little apples,

7 little, 8 little, 9 little apples,

10 little apples all in a row.

Let's go outside

while Mom and Dad prepare.

Rake the leaves.

Jump in the piles!

Wash the apples.

Mix the batter.

Batter up.

Pitch the ball!

10 little, 9 little, 8 little apples,

7 little, 6 little, 5 little apples,

4 little, 3 little, 2 little apples,

1 little apple added to the pie.

Bake in the oven.

Cool on the window.

Something smells good.

Race you inside!

Wash your hands.

Set the table.

The family's together.

We eat our favorite season's treat.